YAKS YAK
Animal Word Pairs
LINDA SUE PARK

ILLUSTRATED BY
JENNIFER BLACK REINHARDT

CLARION BOOKS
HOUGHTON MIFFLIN HARCOURT
BOSTON NEW YORK

Yaks yak.

Bugs bug bugs.

to bug = to annoy

Flounders flounder.

to flounder = to be helpless

Quails quail.

to quail = to shrink away in fear

Apes ape.

to ape = to mimic

Dogs dog dogs.

to dog = to track or follow

Fish fish.

Parrots parrot.

Dapper tie

Dapper tie

Nice hair

Nice hair

Nice hair

Nice hair

silly bird

silly bird

to parrot = to repeat

Bats bat.

to bat = to strike
with a [baseball] bat

to ram = to strike horizontally

oops.

Duck, ducks!

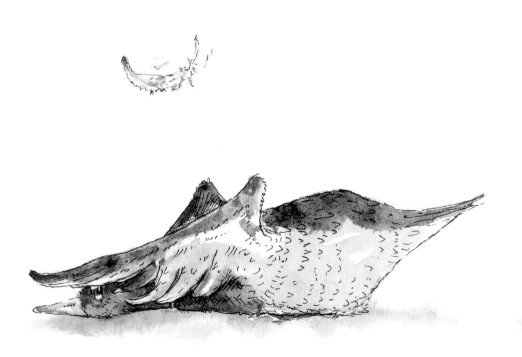

to duck = to crouch or dive

Steers steer.

to steer = to guide

Crows crow.

I'm a rock star

It's good to be me

to crow = to boast

my feathers are the shiniest

my hat is from Paris

I'm the best worm catcher

These are NOT for YOU KEEP AWAY

to hog = to take more than your share

Hogs hog.

Kids kid!

to kid = to tease or joke

The word pairs used in this book are **homographs**—words that are spelled and pronounced the same, but have different meanings.

The Words

	ANIMAL'S NAME	ACTION
yak · to yak	From the Tibetan word for the animal, *g-yag*.	Probably onomatopoetic ("yakkety-yak"), possibly from the Yiddish *yakhne*, meaning busybody.
bug · to bug	Middle English *bugge*, something frightening, possibly related to the Scottish *bogill*, meaning goblin.	First use of *bug* meaning "to annoy or irritate" in the 1940s.
flounder · to flounder	Old North French, *flondre*.	Possibly a variation of *founder*, meaning to collapse or submerge. Also possible: from the Dutch *flodderen*, to flop around.
quail · to quail	From the Old French (*quaille*), or possibly a Germanic source (German *Wachtel*, Dutch *kwakkel*).	To shrink away in fear, from the mid-1500s; usage revived and popularized in the nineteenth century by Sir Walter Scott.
ape · to ape	Old English *apa*, meaning ape or monkey.	From the animal's behavior.
dog · to dog	Old English *docga*, Middle English *dogge*, meaning hound.	From the animal, as in to track or trail someone like a dog.
fish · to fish	Old English *fisc*.	From the animal.
badger · to badger	Possibly from the Anglo-French *bage*, meaning "badge," for the white blaze on its head.	From badger-baiting, a blood sport where dogs and badgers are pitted against each other for entertainment. Outlawed for nearly two centuries, but still practiced illegally in Britain and Ireland.
parrot · to parrot	Sixteenth century, uncertain origin. Possibly derived from the French *perroquet*, meaning parakeet.	From the bird's ability to mimic speech without understanding it.

The Words

	ANIMAL'S NAME	ACTION
bat · to bat	Middle English *bakke*, possibly later confused with the Latin *blatta* (meaning moth or other nocturnal insect).	To strike with a bat, from Old English *batt*, meaning a club or cudgel, the verb deriving from the noun.
slug · to slug	Middle English, from *sluggard*, a lazy or slow person (which in turn comes from Scandinavia: Norwegian *slugga*, Swedish *slogga*).	First use mid-1800s, uncertain origin.
crane · to crane	Old English *cran*, meaning a large wading bird.	From the bird's behavior.
ram · to ram	Old English *ramm*, meaning a male sheep.	From the animal's behavior.
duck · to duck	Old English *duce*, from the verb *ducan*, to duck or dive.	The meaning "to dive" from the bird's behavior. The variant definition "to stoop or bend quickly" first used in the sixteenth century.
steer · to steer	Old English *steor*, young bull.	Old English *steran*, meaning rudder.
crow · to crow	Old English *crawe*, imitating the bird's call.	From the bird's behavior, possibly because it is a carrion eater and squawks triumphantly over its feed.
hog · to hog	Old English *hocg* or *hogg*.	First recorded use 1884, in Mark Twain's *Huckleberry Finn*.
kid · to kid	Old Norse *kiδ*, meaning baby goat. First used to mean "child" in the sixteenth century.	Meaning "to tease or joke" first used mid-nineteeth century, probably from the idea of "acting like a kid."

To Tobin
who gave me the idea
—L.S.P.

Dedicated with love to EMR—your heart always remembers
—J.B.R.

Clarion Books
215 Park Avenue South
New York, New York 10003

Clarion Books is an imprint of Houghton Mifflin Harcourt Publishing Company.

www.hmhco.com

The illustrations in this book were done
in watercolor and ink on Arches 300 lb bright white, hot press, watercolor paper.

The text was set in Bazhonov.
Design by Christine Kettner

Library of Congress Cataloging-in-Publication Data
Names: Park, Linda Sue. | Reinhardt, Jennifer Black, 1963– illustrator.
Title: Yaks yak : animal word Pairs / Linda Sue Park ; illustrated by Jennifer Black Reinhardt.
Description: Boston ; New York : Clarion Books, Houghton Mifflin Harcourt, [2016] | Summary: Presents animals
acting out the verbs made from their names, including hogs hogging, slugs slugging, and other creatures
demonstrating homographs, words with different meanings that are spelled and pronounced the same.
Identifiers: LCCN 2015020003 | ISBN 9780544391017 (hardback)
Subjects: | CYAC: English language—Homonyms—Fiction. | Animals—Fiction. | BISAC: JUVENILE FICTION /
Concepts / Words. | JUVENILE FICTION / Animals / General. | JUVENILE FICTION / Humorous Stories.
Classification: LCC PZ7.P22115 Yak 2016 | DDC [E]—dc23
LC record available at http://lccn.loc.gov/2015020003

Manufactured in Mexico
RDT 10 9 8 7 6 5 4 3 2
4500591825